Pebble® Plus
Bilingüe/
Bilingual

TODO SOBRE EL INVIERNO / ALL ABOUT WINTER

Navidad/Christmas

por/by Martha E. H. Rustad

Editora consultora/Consulting Editor: Gail Saunders-Smith, PhD

CAPSTONE PRESS
a capstone imprint

Pebble Plus is published by Capstone Press,
1710 Roe Crest Drive, North Mankato, Minnesota 56003.
www.capstonepub.com

Library of Congress Cataloging-in-Publication Data
Rustad, Martha E. H. (Martha Elizabeth Hillman), 1975–
  Navidad = Christmas / by Martha E. H. Rustad.
    p. cm.—(Pebble plus todo sobre el invierno/All about winter)
  Includes index.
  Summary: "Simple text and photographs present the winter holiday, Christmas—in both English and
Spanish"—Provided by publisher.
  ISBN 978-1-4296-8240-4 (library binding)
  1. Christmas—Juvenile literature. I. Title. II. Title: Christmas. III. Series.
GT4985.5.R87 2012
394.2663—dc23   2011028791

Editorial Credits
Sarah L. Schuette, editor; Strictly Spanish, translation services; Veronica Correia, designer; Eric Manske,
    bilingual book designer; Marcy Morin, photo shoot scheduler; Kathy McColley, production specialist

Photo Credits
Capstone Press, 7
Capstone Press/Karon Dubke, all (except pg. 7)

Note to Parents and Teachers

The Todo sobre el invierno/All about Winter set supports national science standards
related to changes during the seasons. This book describes and illustrates the winter
holiday, Christmas, in both English and Spanish. The images support early readers in
understanding the text. The repetition of words and phrases helps early readers learn
new words. This book also introduces early readers to subject-specific vocabulary words,
which are defined in the Glossary section. Early readers may need assistance to read
some words and to use the Table of Contents, Glossary, Internet Sites, and Index sections
of the book.

Printed in the United States of America in North Mankato, Minnesota.
112012   007045R

Table of Contents

Tabla de contenidos

Christmas Is Coming!

Christmas Day is on
December 25.
Christians celebrate
the birth of Jesus Christ
on this holiday.

¡Llega la Navidad!

El Día de Navidad es
el 25 de diciembre.
Los cristianos celebran el
nacimiento de Jesucristo
en esta festividad.

Jesus lived more than
2,000 years ago. Jesus
taught people to be kind
and loving to others.

Jesús vivió hace más de
2,000 años. Jesús enseñó
a la gente a ser buena
y a amar a otros.

Getting Ready

We get ready for Christmas
in December. We put up
a tree. We decorate it
with lights and ornaments.

Preparándonos

Nos preparamos para
Navidad en diciembre.
Colocamos un árbol.
Lo decoramos con
luces y adornos.

We shop for presents.
We wrap them and
set them under the
Christmas tree.

Compramos regalos.
Los envolvemos y
colocamos bajo el
árbol de Navidad.

Family Traditions

Grandma Gerry
bakes Christmas cookies.
She decorates them
with frosting and candy.

Tradiciones familiares

Abuela Gerry hornea
galletitas navideñas.
Ella las decora con un
baño y con dulces.

Angela's family
goes to church.
They pray
and sing songs.

———————————————

La familia de Ángela
va a la iglesia.
Ellos rezan y
cantan canciones.

Cord eats with his family.
They have carrots, ham,
and mashed potatoes.

Cord come con su familia.
Ellos comen zanahorias,
jamón y puré de papas.

Santa

Santa is a symbol
of the Christmas spirit.
He reminds people to be
giving all year long.

Santa

Santa es un símbolo del
espíritu navideño. Él recuerda
a la gente a ser generosa
todo el año.

We leave cookies
and milk for Santa
on Christmas Eve.
Merry Christmas!

Dejamos galletitas
y leche para Santa
en Nochebuena.
¡Feliz Navidad!

20

Glossary

celebrate—to do something fun on a special occasion or to mark a major event

decorate—to add items to something to make it prettier; people decorate trees and their homes to celebrate Christmas

holiday—a festival or holy time; people usually take time off work, school, or regular activities during holidays

Jesus Christ—the man Christians worship as the son of God

ornament—a small object used as a decoration

symbol—an object or person that reminds people of something else

Glosario

el adorno—un objeto pequeño usado como decoración

celebrar—hacer algo divertido en una ocasión especial o para marcar un evento importante

decorar—agregar artículos a algo para hacerlo más bonito; gente decora árboles y su hogar para celebrar la Navidad

la festividad—un día festivo o tiempo sagrado; por lo general, la gente se toma días libres del trabajo, de la escuela o actividades regulares durante las fiestas

Jesucristo—el hombre a quien los cristianos adoran como el Hijo de Dios

el símbolo—un objeto o persona que recuerda a la gente de algo

Internet Sites

FactHound offers a safe, fun way to find Internet sites related to this book. All of the sites on FactHound have been researched by our staff.

Here's all you do:

Visit *www.facthound.com*

Type in this code: 9781429682404

Super-cool stuff! Check out projects, games and lots more at **www.capstonekids.com**

Sitios de Internet

FactHound brinda una forma segura y divertida de encontrar sitios de Internet relacionados con este libro. Todos los sitios en FactHound han sido investigados por nuestro personal.

Esto es todo lo que tienes que hacer:

Visita *www.facthound.com*

Ingresa este código: 9781429682404

¡Algo súper divertido! Hay proyectos, juegos y mucho más en **www.capstonekids.com**

Index

Índice